A Stag
in the Bag

Mary Elizabeth Salzmann

Consulting Editor, Diane Craig, M.A./Reading Specialist

ABDO
Publishing Company

Published by ABDO Publishing Company, 4940 Viking Drive, Edina, Minnesota 55435.

Credits
Edited by: Pam Price
Curriculum Coordinator: Nancy Tuminelly
Cover and Interior Design and Production: Mighty Media
Photo Credits: AbleStock, Brand X Pictures, Hemera, Photodisc, Wewerka Photography

Library of Congress Cataloging-in-Publication Data

Salzmann, Mary Elizabeth, 1968-
    A stag in the bag / Mary Elizabeth Salzmann.
        p. cm. -- (First rhymes)
    Includes index.
    ISBN 1-59679-531-X (hardcover)
    ISBN 1-59679-532-8 (paperback)
        1. English language--Rhyme--Juvenile literature. I. Title. II. Series.
    PE1517.S359 2005
    808.1--dc22

                                                                        2005048804

SandCastle™ books are created by a professional team of educators, reading specialists, and content developers around five essential components that include phonemic awareness, phonics, vocabulary, text comprehension, and fluency. All books are written, reviewed, and leveled for guided reading and early intervention reading, and designed for use in shared, guided, and independent reading and writing activities to support a balanced approach to literacy instruction.

Let Us Know

After reading the book, SandCastle would like you to tell us your stories about reading. What is your favorite page? Was there something hard that you needed help with? Share the ups and downs of learning to read. We want to hear from you! To get posted on the ABDO Publishing Company Web site, send us e-mail at:

sandcastle@abdopub.com

SandCastle Level: Beginning

-ag

bag

flag

rag

stag

tag

Look at the  .

Here is the  .

Look at the .

Here is the  .

Look at the .

The bag is brown.

The flag is red,
white, and blue.

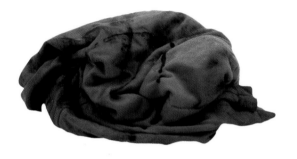

The rag is dirty.

The stag has horns.

The tag has a string.

A Stag in the Bag

One day Dag
found a brown bag.

Dag looked in the bag and saw a small stag.

The stag
from the bag
had a big tag.

Dag,
Rub the stag
with the rag!!

The note on the tag
said to rub the stag
with the rag
that was in the bag.

Dag took the rag
from the bag
and rubbed the stag.

Its tail began to wag
and the tag
turned into a flag!

About SandCastle™

A professional team of educators, reading specialists, and content developers created the SandCastle™ series to support young readers as they develop reading skills and strategies and increase their general knowledge. The SandCastle™ series has four levels that correspond to early literacy development in young children. The levels are provided to help teachers and parents select the appropriate books for young readers.

Emerging Readers
(no flags)

Beginning Readers
(1 flag)

Transitional Readers
(2 flags)

Fluent Readers
(3 flags)

These levels are meant only as a guide. All levels are subject to change.

ABDO
Publishing Company

To see a complete list of SandCastle™ books and other nonfiction titles from ABDO Publishing Company, visit www.abdopub.com or contact us at:
4940 Viking Drive, Edina, Minnesota 55435 • 1-800-800-1312 • fax: 1-952-831-1632